# CERTAIN NOBLE PLAYS OF JAPAN

## LECTOR HOUSE PUBLIC DOMAIN WORKS

# CERTAIN NOBLE PLAYS OF JAPAN

EZRA POUND,
ERNEST FENOLLOSA,
WILLIAM BUTLER YEATS

ISBN: 978-93-5614-677-8

Published: 1916



LECTOR HOUSE

LECTOR HOUSE LLP
E-MAIL: info@lectorhouse.com

# CERTAIN NOBLE PLAYS OF JAPAN

## FROM THE MANUSCRIPTS OF ERNEST FENOLLOSA,

CHOSEN AND FINISHED BY

EZRA POUND

WITH AN INTRODUCTION BY
WILLIAM BUTLER YEATS

TRANSLATED BY
ERNEST FENOLLOSA

MCMXVI

# CONTENTS

# INTRODUCTION

## I

In the series of books I edit for my sister I confine myself to those that have I believe some special value to Ireland, now or in the future. I have asked Mr. Pound for these beautiful plays because I think they will help me to explain a certain possibility of the Irish dramatic movement. I am writing these words with my imagination stirred by a visit to the studio of Mr. Dulac, the distinguished illustrator of the Arabian Nights. I saw there the mask and head-dress to be worn in a play of mine by the player who will speak the part of Cuchulain, and who wearing this noble half-Greek half-Asiatic face will appear perhaps like an image seen in revery by some Orphic worshipper. I hope to have attained the distance from life which can make credible strange events, elaborate words. I have written a little play that can be played in a room for so little money that forty or fifty readers of poetry can pay the price. There will be no scenery, for three musicians, whose seeming sun-burned faces will I hope suggest that they have wandered from village to village in some country of our dreams, can describe place and weather, and at moments action, and accompany it all by drum and gong or flute and dulcimer. Instead of the players working themselves into a violence of passion indecorous in our sitting-room, the music, the beauty of form and voice all come to climax in pantomimic dance.

In fact with the help of these plays 'translated by Ernest Fenollosa and finished by Ezra Pound' I have invented a form of drama, distinguished, indirect and symbolic, and having no need of mob or press to pay its way—an aristocratic form. When this play and its performance run as smoothly as my skill can make them, I shall hope to write another of the same sort and so complete a dramatic celebration of the life of Cuchulain planned long ago. Then having given enough performances for I hope the pleasure of personal friends and a few score people of good taste, I shall record all discoveries of method and turn to something else. It is an advantage of this noble form that it need absorb no one's life, that its few properties can be packed up in a box, or hung upon the walls where they will be fine ornaments.

## II

And yet this simplification is not mere economy. For nearly three centuries invention has been making the human voice and the movements of the body seem always less expressive. I have long been puzzled why passages, that are moving when read out or spoken during rehearsal, seem muffled or dulled during performance. I have simplified scenery, having 'The Hour Glass' for instance played now before green curtains, now among those admirable ivory-coloured screens invented by Gordon Craig. With every simplification the voice has recovered something of its importance and yet when verse has approached in temper to let us say 'Kubla Khan,' or 'The Ode to the West Wind,' the most typical modern verse, I have still felt as if the sound came to me from behind a veil. The stage-opening, the powerful light and shade, the number of feet between myself and the players have destroyed intimacy. I have found myself thinking of players who needed perhaps but to unroll a mat in some Eastern garden. Nor have I felt this only when I listened to speech, but even more when I have watched the movement of a player or heard singing in a play. I love all the arts that can still remind me of their origin among the common people, and my ears are only comfortable when the singer sings as if mere speech had taken fire, when he appears to have passed into song almost imperceptibly. I am bored and wretched, a limitation I greatly regret, when he seems no longer a human being but an invention of science. To explain him to myself I say that he has become a wind instrument and sings no longer like active men, sailor or camel driver, because he has had to compete with an orchestra, where the loudest instrument has always survived. The human voice can only become louder by becoming less articulate, by discovering some new musical sort of roar or scream. As poetry can do neither, the voice must be freed from this competition and find itself among little instruments, only heard at their best perhaps when we are close about them. It should be again possible for a few poets to write as all did once, not for the printed page but to be sung. But movement also has grown less expressive, more declamatory, less intimate. When I called the other day upon a friend I found myself among some dozen people who were watching a group of Spanish boys and girls, professional dancers, dancing some national dance in the midst of a drawing-room. Doubtless their training had been long, laborious and wearisome; but now one could not be deceived, their movement was full of joy. They were among friends, and it all seemed but the play of children; how powerful it seemed, how passionate, while an even more miraculous art, separated from us by the footlights, appeared in the comparison laborious and professional. It is well to be close enough to an artist to feel for him a personal liking, close enough perhaps to feel that our liking is returned.

My play is made possible by a Japanese dancer whom I have seen dance in a studio and in a drawing-room and on a very small stage lit by an excellent stage-light. In the studio and in the drawing-room alone where the lighting was the light we are most accustomed to, did I see him as the tragic image that has stirred my imagination. There where no studied lighting, no stage-picture made an artificial world, he was able, as he rose from the floor, where he had been sitting crossed-legged or as he threw out an arm, to recede from us into some more powerful life. Because that separation was achieved by human means alone, he receded, but to inhabit as it were the deeps of the mind. One realised anew, at every separating strangeness, that the measure of all arts' greatness can be but in their intimacy.

## III

All imaginative art keeps at a distance and this distance once chosen must be firmly held against a pushing world. Verse, ritual, music and dance in association with action require that gesture, costume, facial expression, stage arrangement must help in keeping the door. Our unimaginative arts are content to set a piece of the world as we know it in a place by itself, to put their photographs as it were in a plush or a plain frame, but the arts which interest me, while seeming to separate from the world and us a group of figures, images, symbols, enable us to pass for a few moments into a deep of the mind that had hitherto been too subtle for our habitation. As a deep of the mind can only be approached through what is most human, most delicate, we should distrust bodily distance, mechanism and loud noise.

It may be well if we go to school in Asia, for the distance from life in European art has come from little but difficulty with material. In half-Asiatic Greece, Kallimachos could still return to a stylistic management of the falling folds of drapery, after the naturalistic drapery of Phidias, and in Egypt the same age that saw the village Head-man carved in wood for burial in some tomb with so complete a naturalism saw, set up in public places, statues full of an august formality that implies traditional measurements, a philosophic defence. The spiritual painting of the 14th century passed on into Tintoretto and that of Velasquez into modern painting with no sense of loss to weigh against the gain, while the painting of Japan, not having our European Moon to churn the wits, has understood that no styles that ever delighted noble imaginations have lost their importance, and chooses the style according to the subject. In literature also we have had the illusion of change and progress, the art of Shakespeare passing into that of Dryden, and so into the prose drama, by what has seemed when studied in its details unbroken progress. Had we been Greeks, and so but half-European, an honourable mob would have martyred though in vain the first man who set up a painted scene, or who complained that soliloquies were unnatural, instead of repeating with a sigh, 'we cannot return to the arts of childhood however beautiful.' Only our lyric poetry has kept its Asiatic habit and renewed itself at its own youth, putting off perpetually what has been called its progress in a series of violent revolutions.

Therefore it is natural that I go to Asia for a stage-convention, for more formal faces, for a chorus that has no part in the action and perhaps for those movements of the body copied from the marionette shows of the 14th century. A mask will enable me to substitute for the face of some common-place player, or for that face repainted to suit his own vulgar fancy, the fine invention of a sculptor, and to bring the audience close enough to the play to hear every inflection of the voice. A mask never seems but a dirty face, and no matter how close you go is still a work of art; nor shall we lose by staying the movement of the features, for deep feeling is expressed by a movement of the whole body. In poetical painting & in sculpture the face seems the nobler for lacking curiosity, alert attention, all that we sum up under the famous word of the realists 'vitality.' It is even possible that being is only possessed completely by the dead, and that it is some knowledge of this that makes us gaze with so much emotion upon the face of the Sphinx or Buddha. Who can forget the face of Chaliapine as the Mogul King in Prince Igor, when a mask covering its upper portion made him seem like a Phoenix at the end of its thousand wise years, awaiting in condescension the burning nest and what did it not gain from that immobility in dignity and in power?

## IV

Realism is created for the common people and was always their peculiar delight, and it is the delight to-day of all those whose minds educated alone by school-masters and newspapers are without the memory of beauty and emotional subtlety. The occasional humorous realism that so much heightened the emotional effect of Elizabethan Tragedy, Cleopatra's old man with an asp let us say, carrying the tragic crisis by its contrast above the tide-mark of Corneille's courtly theatre, was made at the outset to please the common citizen standing on the rushes of the floor; but the great speeches were written by poets who remembered their patrons in the covered galleries. The fanatic Savonarola was but dead a century, and his lamentation in the frenzy of his rhetoric, that every prince of the Church or State throughout Europe was wholly occupied with the fine arts, had still its moiety of truth. A poetical passage cannot be understood without a rich memory, and like the older school of painting appeals to a tradition, and that not merely when it speaks of 'Lethe's Wharf' or 'Dido on the wild sea-banks' but in rhythm, in vocabulary; for the ear must notice slight variations upon old cadences and customary words, all that high breeding of poetical style where there is nothing ostentatious, nothing crude, no breath of parvenu or journalist.

Let us press the popular arts on to a more complete realism, for that would be their honesty; and the commercial arts demoralise by their compromise, their incompleteness, their idealism without sincerity or elegance, their pretence that ignorance can understand beauty. In the studio and in the drawing-room we can found a true theatre of beauty. Poets from the time of Keats and Blake have derived their descent only through what is least declamatory, least popular in the art of Shakespeare, and in such a theatre they will find their habitual audience and keep their freedom. Europe is very old and has seen many arts run through the circle and has learned the fruit of every flower and known what this fruit sends up, and it is now time to copy the East and live deliberately.

## V

'Ye shall not, while ye tarry with me, taste
From unrinsed barrel the diluted wine
Of a low vineyard or a plant illpruned,
But such as anciently the Aegean Isles
Poured in libation at their solemn feasts:
And the same goblets shall ye grasp embost
With no vile figures of loose languid boors,
But such as Gods have lived with and have led.'

The Noh theatre of Japan became popular at the close of the 14th century, gathering into itself dances performed at Shinto shrines in honour of spirits and gods or by young nobles at the court, and much old lyric poetry, and receiving its philosophy and its final shape perhaps from priests of a contemplative school of Buddhism. A small daimio or feudal lord of the ancient capital Nara, a contemporary of Chaucer's, was the author, or perhaps only the stage-manager, of many plays. He brought them to the court of the Shogun at Kioto. From that on the Shogun and his court were as busy with dramatic poetry as the Mikado and his with lyric. When for the first time Hamlet was being played in London Noh was made a necessary part of official ceremonies at Kioto, and young nobles and princes, forbidden to attend the popular theatre in Japan as elsewhere a place of mimicry and naturalism were encouraged to witness and to perform in spectacles where speech, music, song and dance created an image of nobility and strange beauty. When the modern revolution came, Noh after a brief unpopularity was played for the first time in certain ceremonious public theatres, and 1897 a battleship was named Takasago, after one of its most famous plays. Some of the old noble families are to-day very poor, their men it may be but servants and labourers, but they still frequent these theatres. 'Accomplishment' the word Noh means, and it is their accomplishment and that of a few cultured people who understand the literary and mythological allusions and the ancient lyrics quoted in speech or chorus, their discipline, a part of their breeding. The players themselves, unlike the despised players of the popular theatre, have passed on proudly from father to son an elaborate art, and even now a player will publish his family tree to prove his skill. One player wrote in 1906 in a business circular—I am quoting from Mr. Pound's redaction of the Notes of Fenollosa—that after thirty generations of nobles a woman of his house dreamed that a mask was carried to her from heaven, and soon after she bore a son who became a player and the father of players. His family he declared still possessed a letter from a 15th century Mikado conferring upon them a theatre-curtain, white below and purple above.

There were five families of these players and, forbidden before the Revolution to perform in public, they had received grants of land or salaries from the state. The white and purple curtain was no doubt to hang upon a wall behind the players or over their entrance door for the Noh stage is a platform surrounded upon three sides by the audience. No 'naturalistic' effect is sought. The players wear masks and found their movements upon those of puppets: the most famous of all Japanese dramatists composed entirely for puppets. A swift or a slow movement and a long or a short stillness, and then another movement. They sing as much as they speak, and there is a chorus which describes the scene and interprets their thought and never becomes as in the Greek theatre a part of the action. At the climax instead of the disordered passion of nature there is a dance, a series of positions & movements which may represent a battle, or a marriage, or the pain of a ghost in the Buddhist purgatory. I have lately studied certain of these dances, with Japanese players, and I notice that their ideal of beauty, unlike that of Greece and like that of pictures from Japan and China, makes them pause at moments of muscular tension. The interest is not in the human form but in the rhythm to which it moves, and the triumph of their art is to express the rhythm in its intensity. There are few swaying movements of arms or body such as make the beauty of our dancing. They move from the hip, keeping constantly the upper part of their body still, and seem to associate with every gesture or pose some definite thought.

They cross the stage with a sliding movement, and one gets the impression not of undulation but of continuous straight lines.

The Print Room of the British Museum is now closed as a war-economy, so I can only write from memory of theatrical colour-prints, where a ship is represented by a mere skeleton of willows or osiers painted green, or a fruit tree by a bush in a pot, and where actors have tied on their masks with ribbons that are gathered into a bunch behind the head. It is a child's game become the most noble poetry, and there is no observation of life, because the poet would set before us all those things which we feel and imagine in silence.

Mr. Ezra Pound has found among the Fenollosa manuscripts a story traditional among Japanese players. A young man was following a stately old woman through the streets of a Japanese town, and presently she turned to him and spoke: 'Why do you follow me?' 'Because you are so interesting.' 'That is not so, I am too old to be interesting.' But he wished he told her to become a player of old women on the Noh stage. 'If he would become famous as a Noh player she said, he must not observe life, nor put on an old voice and stint the music of his voice. He must know how to suggest an old woman and yet find it all in the heart.'

## VI

In the plays themselves I discover a beauty or a subtlety that I can trace perhaps to their threefold origin. The love-sorrows, the love of father and daughter, of mother and son, of boy and girl, may owe their nobility to a courtly life, but he to whom the adventures happen, a traveller commonly from some distant place, is most often a Buddhist priest; and the occasional intellectual subtlety is perhaps Buddhist. The adventure itself is often the meeting with ghost, god or goddess at some holy place or much-legended tomb; and god, goddess or ghost reminds me at times of our own Irish legends and beliefs, which once it may be differed little from those of the Shinto worshipper.

The feather-mantle, for whose lack the moon goddess, (or should we call her fairy?) cannot return to the sky, is the red cap whose theft can keep our fairies of the sea upon dry land; and the ghost-lovers in 'Nishikigi' remind me of the Aran boy and girl who in Lady Gregory's story come to the priest after death to be married. These Japanese poets too feel for tomb and wood the emotion, the sense of awe that our Gaelic speaking country people will some times show when you speak to them of Castle Hackett or of some Holy Well; and that is why perhaps it pleases them to begin so many plays by a Traveller asking his way with many questions, a convention agreeable to me; for when I first began to write poetical plays for an Irish theatre I had to put away an ambition of helping to bring again to certain places, their old sanctity or their romance. I could lay the scene of a play on Baile's Strand, but I found no pause in the hurried action for descriptions of strand or sea or the great yew tree that once stood there; and I could not in 'The King's Threshold' find room, before I began the ancient story, to call up the shallow river and the few trees and rocky fields of modern Gort. But in the 'Nishikigi' the tale of the lovers would lose its pathos if we did not see that forgotten tomb where 'the hiding fox' lives among 'the orchids and the chrysanthemum flowers.' The men who created this convention were more like ourselves than were the Greeks and Romans, more like us even than are Shakespeare and Corneille. Their emotion was self-conscious and reminiscent, always associating itself with pictures and poems. They measured all that time had taken or would take away and found their delight in remembering celebrated lovers in the scenery pale passion loves. They travelled seeking for the strange and for the picturesque: 'I go about with my heart set upon no particular place, no more than a cloud. I wonder now would the sea be that way, or the little place Kefu that they say is stuck down against it.' When a traveller asks his way of girls upon the roadside he is directed to find it by certain pine trees, which he will recognise because many people have drawn them.

I wonder am I fanciful in discovering in the plays themselves (few examples have as yet been translated and I may be misled by accident or the idiosyncrasy of some poet) a playing upon a single metaphor, as deliberate as the echoing rhythm of line in Chinese and Japanese painting. In the 'Nishikigi' the ghost of the girl-lover carries the cloth she went on weaving out of grass when she should have opened the chamber door to her lover, and woven grass returns again and again in metaphor and incident. The lovers, now that in an aery body they must sorrow for unconsummated love, are 'tangled up as the grass patterns are tangled.' Again they are like an unfinished cloth: 'these bodies, having no weft, even now are not come together, truly a shameful story, a tale to bring shame on the gods.' Before they can bring the priest to the tomb they spend the day 'pushing aside the grass from the overgrown ways in Kefu,' and the countryman who directs them is 'cutting grass on the hill;' & when at last the prayer of the priest unites them in marriage the bride says that he has made 'a dream-bridge over wild grass, over the grass I dwell in;' and in the end bride and bridegroom show themselves for a moment 'from under the shadow of the love-grass.'

In 'Hagoromo' the feather-mantle of the fairy woman creates also its rhythm of metaphor. In the beautiful day of opening spring 'the plumage of Heaven drops neither feather nor flame,' 'nor is the rock of earth over-much worn by the brushing of the feathery skirt of the stars.' One half remembers a thousand Japanese paintings, or whichever comes first into the memory. That screen painted by Korin, let us say, shown lately at the British Museum, where the same form is echoing in wave and in cloud and in rock. In European poetry I remember Shelley's continually repeated fountain and cave, his broad stream and solitary star. In neglecting character which seems to us essential in drama, as do their artists in neglecting relief and depth, when they arrange flowers in a vase in a thin row, they have made possible a hundred lovely intricacies.

## VII

These plays arose in an age of continual war and became a part of the education of soldiers. These soldiers, whose natures had as much of Walter Pater as of Achilles combined with Buddhist priests and women to elaborate life in a ceremony, the playing of football, the drinking of tea, and all great events of state, becoming a ritual. In the painting that decorated their walls and in the poetry they recited one discovers the only sign of a great age that cannot deceive us, the most vivid and subtle discrimination of sense and the invention of images more powerful than sense; the continual presence of reality. It is still true that the Deity gives us, according to His promise, not His thoughts or His convictions but His flesh and blood, and I believe that the elaborate technique of the arts, seeming to create out of itself a superhuman life has taught more men to die than oratory or the Prayer Book. We only believe in those thoughts which have been conceived not in the brain but in the whole body. The Minoan soldier who bore upon his arm the shield ornamented with the dove in the Museum at Crete, or had upon his head the helmet with the winged horse, knew his rôle in life. When Nobuzane painted the child Saint Kobo, Daishi kneeling full of sweet austerity upon the flower of the lotus, he set up before our eyes exquisite life and the acceptance of death.

I cannot imagine those young soldiers and the women they loved pleased with the ill-breeding and theatricality of Carlyle, nor I think with the magniloquence of Hugo. These things belong to an industrial age, a mechanical sequence of ideas; but when I remember that curious game which the Japanese called, with a confusion of the senses that had seemed typical of our own age, 'listening to incense,' I know that some among them would have understood the prose of Walter Pater, the painting or Puvis de Chavannes, the poetry of Mallarmé and Verlaine. When heroism returned to our age it bore with it as its first gift technical sincerity.

## VIII

For some weeks now I have been elaborating my play in London where alone I can find the help I need, Mr. Dulac's mastery of design and Mr. Ito's genius of movement; yet it pleases me to think that I am working for my own country. Perhaps some day a play in the form I am adapting for European purposes shall awake once more, whether in Gaelic or in English, under the slope of Slieve-namon or Croagh Patrick ancient memories; for this form has no need of scenery that runs away with money nor of a theatre-building. Yet I know that I only amuse myself with a fancy; for though my writings if they be sea-worthy must put to sea, I cannot tell where they may be carried by the wind. Are not the fairy-stories of Oscar Wilde, which were written for Mr. Ricketts and Mr. Shannon and for a few ladies, very popular in Arabia?

W. B. Yeats, April 1916.

# NISHIKIGI

## A PLAY IN TWO ACTS

BY

MOTOKIYO

## NISHIKIGI,
## A PLAY IN TWO ACTS
## BY
## MOTOKIYO.

### PERSONS OF THE PLAY

| | |
|---|---|
| THE WAKI | A priest |
| THE SHITE, OR HERO | Ghost of the lover |
| TSURE | Ghost of the woman; they have both been long dead, and have not yet been united. |
| CHORUS | |

The 'Nishikigi' are wands used as a love charm. 'Hosonuno' is the name of a local cloth which the woman weaves.

# NISHIKIGI

## FIRST PART

**WAKI**

There never was anybody heard of Mount Shinobu but had a kindly feeling for it; so I, like any other priest that might want to know a little bit about each one of the provinces, may as well be walking up here along the much travelled road.

I have not yet been about the east country, but now I have set my mind to go as far as the earth goes; and why shouldn't I, after all? seeing that I go about with my heart set upon no particular place whatsoever, and with no other man's flag in my hand, no more than a cloud has. It is a flag of the night I see coming down upon me. I wonder now, would the sea be that way, or the little place Kefu that they say is stuck down against it?

**SHITE (to Tsure)**

Times out of mind am I here setting up this bright branch, this silky wood with the charms painted in it as fine as the web you'd get in the grass-cloth of Shinobu, that they'd be still selling you in this mountain.

**SHITE AND TSURE**

Tangled, we are entangled. Whose fault was it, dear? tangled up as the grass patterns are tangled up in this coarse cloth, or as the little Mushi that lives on and chirrups in dried sea-weed. We do not know where are to-day our tears in the undergrowth of this eternal wilderness. We neither wake nor sleep, and passing our nights in a sorrow which is in the end a vision, what are these scenes of spring to us? This thinking in sleep of someone who has no thought of you, is it more than a dream? and yet surely it is the natural way of love. In our hearts there is much and in our bodies nothing, and we do nothing at all, and only the waters of the river of tears flow quickly.

**CHORUS**

Narrow is the cloth of Kefu, but wild is that river, that torrent of the hills, between the beloved and the bride.

The cloth she had woven is faded, the thousand one hundred nights were night-trysts watched out in vain.

**WAKI (not recognizing the nature of the speakers)**

Strange indeed, seeing these town-people here.
They seem like man and wife,

And the lady seems to be holding something
Like a cloth woven of feathers,
While he has a staff or a wooden sceptre
Beautifully ornate.
Both of these things are strange;
In any case, I wonder what they call them.

**TSURE**

This is a narrow cloth called 'Hosonuno,'
It is just the breadth of the loom.

**SHITE**

And this is merely wood painted,
And yet the place is famous because of these things.
Would you care to buy them from us?

**WAKI**

Yes, I know that the cloth of this place and the lacquers are famous things. I have already heard of their glory, and yet I still wonder why they have such great reputation.

**TSURE**

Ah well now, that's a disappointment. Here they call the wood 'Nishikigi,' and the woven stuff 'Hosonuno,' and yet you come saying that you have never heard why, and never heard the story. Is it reasonable?

**SHITE**

No, no, that is reasonable enough. What can people be expected to know of these affairs when it is more than they can do to keep abreast of their own?

**BOTH (to the Priest)**

Ah well, you look like a person who has abandoned the world; it is reasonable enough that you should not know the worth of wands and cloths with love's signs painted upon them, with love's marks painted and dyed.

**WAKI**

That is a fine answer. And you would tell me then that Nishikigi and Hosonuno are names bound over with love?

**SHITE**

They are names in love's list surely. Every day for a year, for three years come to their full, the wands Nishikigi were set up, until there were a thousand in all. And they are in song in your time, and will be. 'Chidzuka' they call them.

**TSURE**

These names are surely a by-word.
As the cloth Hosonuno is narrow of weft,
More narrow than the breast,
We call by this name any woman

Whose breasts are hard to come nigh to.
It is a name in books of love.

**SHITE**

'Tis a sad name to look back on.

**TSURE**

A thousand wands were in vain.
A sad name, set in a story.

**SHITE**

A seed-pod void of the seed,
We had no meeting together.

**TSURE**

Let him read out the story.

**CHORUS**

I

At last they forget, they forget.
The wands are no longer offered,
The custom is faded away.
The narrow cloth of Kefu
Will not meet over the breast.
'Tis the story of Hosonuno,
This is the tale:
These bodies, having no weft,
Even now are not come together.
Truly a shameful story,
A tale to bring shame on the gods.

II

Names of love,
Now for a little spell,
For a faint charm only,
For a charm as slight as the binding together
Of pine-flakes in Iwashiro,
And for saying a wish over them about sunset,
We return, and return to our lodging.
The evening sun leaves a shadow.

**WAKI**

Go on, tell out all the story.

**SHITE**

There is an old custom of this country. We make wands of meditation, and deck them with symbols, and set them before a gate, when we are suitors.

**TSURE**

And we women take up a wand of the man we would meet with, and let the others lie, although a man might come for a hundred nights, it may be, or for a thousand nights in three years, till there were a thousand wands here in the shade of this mountain. We know the funeral cave of such a man, one who had watched out the thousand nights; a bright cave, for they buried him with all his wands. They have named it the 'Cave of the many charms.'

**WAKI**

I will go to that love-cave,
It will be a tale to take back to my village.
Will you show me my way there?

**SHITE**

So be it, I will teach you the path.

**TSURE**

Tell him to come over this way.

**BOTH**

Here are the pair of them
Going along before the traveller.

**CHORUS**

We have spent the whole day until dusk
Pushing aside the grass
From the over-grown way at Kefu,
And we are not yet come to the cave.
O you there, cutting grass on the hill,
Please set your mind on this matter.
'You'd be asking where the dew is
'While the frost's lying here on the road.
'Who'd tell you that now?'
Very well then don't tell us,
But be sure we will come to the cave.

**SHITE**

There's a cold feel in the autumn.
Night comes....

**CHORUS**

And storms; trees giving up their leaf,
Spotted with sudden showers.
Autumn! our feet are clogged
In the dew-drenched, entangled leaves.
The perpetual shadow is lonely,
The mountain shadow is lying alone.
The owl cries out from the ivies

That drag their weight on the pine.
Among the orchids and chrysanthemum flowers
The hiding fox is now lord of that love-cave,
Nishidzuka,
That is dyed like the maple's leaf.
They have left us this thing for a saying.
That pair have gone into the cave.
(sign for the exit of Shite and Tsure)

## SECOND PART

(The Waki has taken the posture of sleep. His respectful visit to the cave is beginning to have its effect.)

**WAKI (restless)**

It seems that I cannot sleep
For the length of a pricket's horn.
Under October wind, under pines, under night!
I will do service to Butsu.
(he performs the gestures of a ritual)

**TSURE**

Aie! honoured priest!
You do not dip twice in the river
Beneath the same tree's shadow
Without bonds in some other life.
Hear sooth-say,
Now is there meeting between us,
Between us who were until now
In life and in after-life kept apart.
A dream-bridge over wild grass,
Over the grass I dwell in.
O honoured! do not awake me by force.
I see that the law is perfect.

**SHITE (supposedly invisible)**

It is a good service you have done, sir,
A service that spreads in two worlds,
And binds up an ancient love
That was stretched out between them.
I had watched for a thousand days.
Take my thanks,
For this meeting is under a difficult law.
And now I will show myself in the form of Nishikigi.
I will come out now for the first time in colour.

(The characters announce or explain their acts, as these are mostly symbolical. Thus here the Shite, or Sh'te, announces his change of costume, and later the dance.)

**CHORUS**

The three years are over and past:
All that is but an old story.

**SHITE**

To dream under dream we return.
Three years.... And the meeting comes now!
This night has happened over and over,
And only now comes the tryst.

**CHORUS**

Look there to the cave
Beneath the stems of the Suzuki.
From under the shadows of the love-grass,
See, see how they come forth and appear
For an instant.... Illusion!

**SHITE**

There is at the root of hell
No distinction between princes and commons;
Wretched for me! 'tis the saying.

**WAKI**

Strange, what seemed so very old a cave
Is all glittering-bright within,
Like the flicker of fire.
It is like the inside of a house.
They are setting up a loom,
And heaping up charm-sticks. No,
The hangings are out of old time.
Is it illusion, illusion?

**TSURE**

Our hearts have been in the dark of the falling snow,
We have been astray in the flurry.
You should tell better than we
How much is illusion;
You who are in the world.
We have been in the whirl of those who are fading.

**SHITE**

Indeed in old times Narihira said,
—and he has vanished with the years—
'Let a man who is in the world tell the fact.'
It is for you, traveller,
To say how much is illusion.

**WAKI**

Let it be a dream, or a vision,
Or what you will, I care not.
Only show me the old times over-past and snowed under—
Now, soon, while the night lasts.

**SHITE**

Look then, the old times are shown,
Faint as the shadow-flower shows in the grass that bears it;
And you've but a moon for lanthorn.

**TSURE**

The woman has gone into the cave.
She sets up her loom there
For the weaving of Hosonuno,
Thin as the heart of Autumn.

**SHITE**

The suitor for his part, holding his charm-sticks,
Knocks on a gate which was barred.

**TSURE**

In old time he got back no answer,
No secret sound at all
Save....

**SHITE**

The sound of the loom.

**TSURE**

It was a sweet sound like katydids and crickets,
A thin sound like the Autumn.

**SHITE**

It was what you would hear any night.

**TSURE**

Kiri.

**SHITE**

Hatari.

**TSURE**

Cho.

**SHITE**

Cho.

**CHORUS (mimicking the sound of crickets)**

Kiri, hatari, cho, cho,

Kiri, hatari, cho, cho.
The cricket sews on at his old rags,
With all the new grass in the field; sho,
Churr, isho, like the whir of a loom: churr.

**CHORUS (antistrophe)**

Let be, they make grass-cloth in Kefu,
Kefu, the land's end, matchless in the world.

**SHITE**

That is an old custom, truly,
But this priest would look on the past.

**CHORUS**

The good priest himself would say:
Even if we weave the cloth, Hosonuno,
And set up the charm-sticks
For a thousand, a hundred nights,
Even then our beautiful desire will not pass,
Nor fade nor die out.

**SHITE**

Even to-day the difficulty of our meeting is remembered,
And is remembered in song.

**CHORUS**

That we may acquire power,
Even in our faint substance,
We will show forth even now,
And though it be but in a dream,
Our form of repentance.
(explaining the movement of the Shite and Tsure)
There he is carrying wands,
And she has no need to be asked.
See her within the cave,
With a cricket-like noise of weaving.
The grass-gates and the hedge are between them;
That is a symbol.
Night has already come on.
(now explaining the thoughts of the man's spirit)
Love's thoughts are heaped high within him,
As high as the charm-sticks,
As high as the charm-sticks, once coloured,
Now fading, lie heaped in this cave.
And he knows of their fading. He says:
I lie a body, unknown to any other man,
Like old wood buried in moss.
It were a fit thing

That I should stop thinking the love-thoughts.
The charm-sticks fade and decay,
And yet,
The rumour of our love
Takes foot and moves through the world.
We had no meeting
But tears have, it seems, brought out a bright blossom
Upon the dyed tree of love.

**SHITE**
Tell me, could I have foreseen
Or known what a heap of my writings
Should lie at the end of her shaft-bench?

**CHORUS**
A hundred nights and more
Of twisting, encumbered sleep,
And now they make it a ballad,
Not for one year or for two only
But until the days lie deep
As the sand's depth at Kefu,
Until the year's end is red with Autumn,
Red like these love-wands,
A thousand nights are in vain.
And I stand at this gate-side.
You grant no admission, you do not show yourself
Until I and my sleeves are faded.
By the dew-like gemming of tears upon my sleeve,
Why will you grant no admission?
And we all are doomed to pass,
You, and my sleeves and my tears.
And you did not even know when three years had come to an end.
Cruel, ah cruel!
The charm-sticks....

**SHITE**
Were set up a thousand times;
Then, now, and for always.

**CHORUS**
Shall I ever at last see into that room of hers, which no other sight has traversed?

**SHITE**
Happy at last and well-starred,
Now comes the eve of betrothal:
We meet for the wine-cup.

**CHORUS**

How glorious the sleeves of the dance,
That are like snow-whirls!

**SHITE**

Tread out the dance.

**CHORUS**

Tread out the dance and bring music.
This dance is for Nishikigi.

**SHITE**

This dance is for the evening plays,
And for the weaving.

**CHORUS**

For the tokens between lover and lover:
It is a reflecting in the wine-cup.

**CHORUS**

Ari-aki,
The dawn!
Come, we are out of place;
Let us go ere the light comes.
(to the Waki)
We ask you, do not awake,
We all will wither away,
The wands and this cloth of a dream.
Now you will come out of sleep,
You tread the border and nothing
Awaits you: no, all this will wither away.
There is nothing here but this cave in the field's midst.
To-day's wind moves in the pines;
A wild place, unlit, and unfilled.

# HAGOROMO

## A PLAY IN ONE ACT

## HAGOROMO,
## A PLAY IN ONE ACT

### PERSONS OF THE PLAY

| | |
|---|---|
| THE PRIEST | Hakuryo |
| A FISHERMAN | |
| A TENNIN | |
| CHORUS | |

# HAGOROMO

The plot of the play 'Hagoromo, the Feather-mantle' is as follows. The priest finds the Hagoromo, the magical feather-mantle of a Tennin, an aerial spirit or celestial dancer, hanging upon a bough. She demands its return. He argues with her, and finally promises to return it, if she will teach him her dance or part of it. She accepts the offer. The Chorus explains the dance as symbolical of the daily changes of the moon. The words about 'three, five and fifteen' refer to the number of nights in the moon's changes. In the finale, the Tennin is supposed to disappear like a mountain slowly hidden in mist. The play shows the relation of the early Noh to the God-dance.

**PRIEST**

Windy road of the waves by Miwo,
Swift with ships, loud over steersmen's voices.
Hakuryo, taker of fish, head of his house,
Dwells upon the barren pine-waste of Miwo.

**A FISHERMAN**

Upon a thousand heights had gathered the inexplicable cloud, swept by the rain. The moon is just come to light the low house. A clean and pleasant time surely. There comes the breath-colour of spring; the waves rise in a line below the early mist; the moon is still delaying above, though we've no skill to grasp it. Here is a beauty to set the mind above itself.

**CHORUS**

I shall not be out of memory
Of the mountain road by Kiyomi,
Nor of the parted grass by that bay,
Nor of the far-seen pine-waste
Of Miwo of wheat stalks.

Let us go according to custom. Take hands against the wind here, for it presses the clouds and the sea. Those men who were going to fish are about to return without launching. Wait a little, is it not spring? will not the wind be quiet? this wind is only the voice of the lasting pine-trees, ready for stillness. See how the air is soundless, or would be, were it not for the waves. There now, the fishermen are putting out with even the smallest boats.

**PRIEST**

Now I am come to shore at Miwo-no; I disembark in Subara; I see all that they speak of on the shore. An empty sky with music, a rain of flowers, strange fragrance on every side; all these are no common things, nor is this cloak that hangs upon the pine-tree. As I approach to inhale its colour I am aware of mystery. Its colour-smell is mysterious. I see that it is surely no common dress. I will take it now and return and make it a treasure in my house, to show to the aged.

**TENNIN**

That cloak belongs to someone on this side. What are you proposing to do with it?

**PRIEST**

This? this is a cloak picked up. I am taking it home, I tell you.

**TENNIN**

That is a feather-mantle not fit for a mortal to bear,
Not easily wrested from the sky-traversing spirit,
Not easily taken or given.
I ask you to leave it where you found it.

**PRIEST**

How, is the owner of this cloak a Tennin? so be it. In this downcast age I should keep it, a rare thing, and make it a treasure in the country, a thing respected. Then I should not return it.

**TENNIN**

Pitiful, there is no flying without the cloak of feathers, no return through the ether. I pray you return me the mantle.

**PRIEST**

Just from hearing these high words, I, Hakuryo have gathered more and yet more force. You think, because I was too stupid to recognise it, that I shall be unable to take and keep hid the feather-robe, that I shall give it back for merely being told to stand and withdraw?

**TENNIN**

A Tennin without her robe,
A bird without wings,
How shall she climb the air?

**PRIEST**

And this world would be a sorry place for her to dwell in?

**TENNIN**

I am caught, I struggle, how shall I?...

**PRIEST**

No, Hakuryo is not one to give back the robe.

**TENNIN**

Power does not attain....

**PRIEST**

To get back the robe.

**CHORUS**

Her coronet[1] jewelled as with the dew of tears, even the flowers that decorated her hair drooping, and fading, the whole chain of weaknesses[2] of the dying Tennin can be seen actually before the eyes. Sorrow!

**TENNIN**

I look into the flat of heaven, peering; the cloud-road is all hidden and uncertain; we are lost in the rising mist; I have lost the knowledge of the road. Strange, a strange sorrow!

**CHORUS**

Enviable colour of breath, wonder of clouds that fade along the sky that was our accustomed dwelling; hearing the sky-bird, accustomed and well accustomed, hearing the voices grow fewer, the wild geese fewer and fewer along the highways of air, how deep her longing to return. Plover and seagull are on the waves in the offing. Do they go, or do they return? She reaches out for the very blowing of the spring wind against heaven.

**PRIEST (to the Tennin)**

What do you say? now that I can see you in your sorrow, gracious, of heaven, I bend and would return you your mantle.

**TENNIN**

It grows clearer. No, give it this side.

**PRIEST**

First tell me your nature, who are you, Tennin? give payment with the dance of the Tennin, and I will return you your mantle.

**TENNIN**

Readily and gladly, and then I return into heaven. You shall have what pleasure you will, and I will leave a dance here, a joy to be new among men and to be memorial dancing. Learn then this dance that can turn the palace of the moon. No, come here to learn it. For the sorrows of the world I will leave this new dancing with you for sorrowful people. But give me my mantle, I cannot do the dance rightly without it.

---

[1] Vide examples of state head-dress of kingfisher feathers, in the South Kensington Museum.

[2] The chain of weaknesses, or the five ills, diseases of the Tennin: namely, the hanakadzusa withers; the Hagoromo is stained; sweat comes from the body; both eyes wink frequently; she feels very weary of her palace in heaven.

**PRIEST**

Not yet, for if you should get it, how do I know you'll not be off to your palace without even beginning your dance, not even a measure?

**TENNIN**

Doubt is fitting for mortals; with us there is no deceit.

**PRIEST**

I am again ashamed. I give you your mantle.

**CHORUS**

The young maid now is arrayed; she assumes the curious mantle; watch how she moves in the dance of the rainbow-feathered garment.

**PRIEST**

The heavenly feather-robe moves in accord with the wind.

**TENNIN**

The sleeves of flowers are being wet with the rain.

**PRIEST**

The wind and the sleeve move together.

**CHORUS**

It seems that she dances.
Thus was the dance of pleasure,
Suruga dancing, brought to the sacred east.
Thus was it when the lords of the everlasting
Trod the world,
They being of old our friends.
Upon ten sides their sky is without limit,
They have named it on this account, 'the enduring.'

**TENNIN**

The jewelled axe takes up the eternal renewing, the palace of the moon-god is being renewed with the jewelled axe, and this is always recurring.

**CHORUS (commenting on the dance)**

The white kiromo, the black kiromo,
Three, five into fifteen,
The figure that the Tennin is dividing.
There are heavenly nymphs, Amaotome,[3]
One for each night of the month,
And each with her deed assigned.

**TENNIN**

I also am heaven-born and a maid, Amaotome. Of them there are many. This

[3] Cf. 'Paradiso,' xxiii, 25. 'Quale nei plenilunii sereni Trivia ride tra le ninfe eterne.'

is the dividing of my body, that is fruit of the moon's tree, Katsuma.[4] This is one part of our dance that I leave to you here in your world.

**CHORUS**

The spring mist is widespread abroad; so perhaps the wild olive's flower will blossom in the infinitely unreachable moon. Her flowery head-ornament is putting on colour; this truly is sign of the spring. Not sky is here, but the beauty; and even here comes the heavenly, wonderful wind. O blow, shut the accustomed path of the clouds. O, you in the form of a maid, grant us the favour of your delaying. The pine-waste of Miwo puts on the colour of spring. The bay of Kiyomi lies clear before the snow upon Fuji. Are not all these presages of the spring? There are but few ripples beneath the piny wind. It is quiet along the shore. There is naught but a fence of jewels between the earth and the sky, and the gods within and without,[5] beyond and beneath the stars, and the moon unclouded by her lord, and we who are born of the sun. This alone intervenes, here where the moon is unshadowed, here in Nippon, the sun's field.

**TENNIN**

The plumage of heaven drops neither feather nor flame to its own diminution.

**CHORUS**

Nor is this rock of earth over-much worn by the brushing of that feather-mantle, the feathery skirt of the stars: rarely, how rarely. There is a magic song from the east, the voices of many and many: and flute and shae, filling the space beyond the cloud's edge, seven-stringed; dance filling and filling. The red sun blots on the sky the line of the colour-drenched mountains. The flowers rain in a gust; it is no racking storm that comes over this green moor, which is afloat, as it would seem, in these waves. Wonderful is the sleeve of the white cloud, whirling such snow here.

**TENNIN**

Plain of life, field of the sun, true foundation, great power!

**CHORUS**

Hence and for ever this dancing shall be called, 'a revel in the east.' Many are the robes thou hast, now of the sky's colour itself, and now a green garment.

**SEMI-CHORUS**

And now the robe of mist, presaging spring, a colour-smell as this wonderful maiden's skirt—left, right, left! The rustling of flowers, the putting-on of the feathery sleeve; they bend in air with the dancing.

**SEMI-CHORUS**

Many are the joys in the east. She who is the colour-person of the moon takes her middle-night in the sky. She marks her three fives with this dancing, as a shadow of all fulfilments. The circled vows are at full. Give the seven jewels of rain and all of the treasure, you who go from us. After a little time, only a little time, can

[4] A tree something like the laurel.

[5] 'Within and without,' gei, gu, two parts of the temple.

the mantle be upon the wind that was spread over Matsubara or over Ashilaka the mountain, though the clouds lie in its heaven like a plain awash with sea. Fuji is gone; the great peak of Fuji is blotted out little by little. It melts into the upper mist. In this way she (the Tennin) is lost to sight.

# KUMASAKA
## A PLAY IN TWO ACTS

**BY**

**UJINOBU,**

ADOPTED SON OF MOTOKIJO

# KUMASAKA,
# A PLAY IN TWO ACTS
# BY
# UJINOBU, ADOPTED SON OF MOTOKIJO.

## PERSONS OF THE PLAY

| | |
|---|---|
| A PRIEST | |
| FIRST SHITE, OR HERO | The apparition of Kumasaka in the form of an old priest |
| SECOND SHITE | The apparition of Kumasaka in his true form. |
| CHORUS | This chorus sometimes speaks what the chief characters are thinking, sometimes it describes or interprets the meaning of their movements. |
| | Plot: the ghost of Kumasaka makes reparation for his brigandage by protecting the country. He comes back to praise the bravery of the young man who killed him in single combat. |

# KUMASAKA

## FIRST PART

**PRIEST**

Where shall I rest, wandering, weary of the world? I am a city-bred priest, I have not seen the east counties, and I've a mind to go there. Crossing the hills, I look on the lake of Omi, on the woods of Awatsu. Going over the long bridge at Seta, I rested a night at Noje, and another at Shinohara, and at the dawn I came to the green field, Awono in Miwo. I now pass Akasaka at sunset.

**SHITE (In the form of an old priest)**

I could tell that priest a thing or two.

**PRIEST**

Do you mean me, what is it?

**SHITE**

A certain man died on this day. I ask you to pray for him.

**PRIEST**

All right, but for whom shall I pray?

**SHITE**

I will not tell you his name, but his grave lies in the green field beyond that tall pine tree. He cannot enter to the gates of Paradise, and so I ask you to pray.

**PRIEST**

But I do not think it is proper to pray unless you tell me his name.

**SHITE**

No, no; you can pray the prayer, Ho kai shijo biodo riaku; that would do.

**PRIEST (praying)**

Unto all mortals let there be equal grace, to pass from this life of agony by the gates of death into law, into the peaceful kingdom.

**SHITE (saying first a word or two)**

If you pray for him,—

**CHORUS (continuing the sentence)**

If you pray with the prayer of 'Exeat' he will be thankful, and you need not be aware of his name. They say that prayer can be heard for even the grass and the plants, for even the sand and the soil here; and they will surely hear it, if you pray for an unknown man.

**SHITE**

Will you enter? This is my cottage.

**PRIEST**

This is your house? Very well, I will hold the service in your house; but I see no picture of Buddha nor any wooden image in this cottage, nothing but a long spear on one wall and an iron stick in place of a priest's wand, and many arrows. What are these for?

**SHITE (thinking)**

Yes, this priest is still in the first stage of faith. (aloud) As you see, there are many villages here: Zorii, Awohaka, and Akasaka. But the tall grass of Awo-no-ga-kara grows round the roads between them, and the forest is thick at Koyasu and Awohaka, and many robbers come out under the rains. They attack the baggage on horseback, and take the clothing of maids and servants who pass here. So I go out with this spear.

**PRIEST**

That's very fine, isn't it?

**CHORUS**

You will think it very strange for a priest to do this; but even Buddha has the sharp sword of Mida, and Aijen Miowo has arrows, and Tamon, taking his long spear, throws down the evil spirits.

**SHITE**

The deep love.

**CHORUS**

—is excellent. Good feeling and keeping order are much more excellent than the love of Bosatsu. 'I think of these matters and know little of anything else. It is from my own heart that I am lost, wandering. But if I begin talking I shall keep on talking until dawn. Go to bed, good father; I will sleep too.' He seemed to be going to his bedroom, but suddenly his figure disappeared, and the cottage became a field of grass. The priest passes the night under the pine trees.

**PRIEST**

I cannot sleep out the night. Perhaps if I held my service during the night under this pine tree....

(He begins his service for the dead man.)

## SECOND PART

**SECOND SHITE**

There are winds in the east and south; the clouds are not calm in the west; and in the north the wind of the dark evening blusters; and under the shade of the mountain—

**CHORUS**

There is a rustling of boughs and leaves.

**SECOND SHITE**

Perhaps there will be moon-shine to-night, but the clouds veil the sky; the moon will not break up their shadow. 'Have at them!' 'Ho there!' 'Dash in!' That is the way I would shout, calling and ordering my men before and behind, my bowmen and horsemen. I plundered men of their treasure, that was my work in the world, and now I must go on; it is sorry work for a spirit.

**PRIEST**

Are you Kumasaka Chohan? Tell me the tale of your years.

**SECOND SHITE (now known as Kumasaka)**

There were great merchants in Sanjo, Yoshitsugu, and Nobutaka; they collected treasure each year; they sent rich goods up to Oku. It was then I assailed their trains. Would you know what men were with me?

**PRIEST**

Tell me the chief men, were they from many a province?

**KUMASAKA**

There was Kakusho of Kawachi, there were the two brothers Suriharitaro; they have no rivals in fencing. (omotenchi, face to face attack)

**PRIEST**

What chiefs came to you from the city?

**KUMASAKA**

Emoi of Sanjo, Kozari of Mibu.

**PRIEST**

In the fighting with torches and in mêlée—

**KUMASAKA**

They had no equals.

**PRIEST**

In northern Hakoku?

**KUMASAKA**

Were Aso no Matsuwaka and Mikune no Kure.

**PRIEST**
In Kaga?

**KUMASAKA**
No, Chohan was the head there. There were seventy comrades who were very strong and skilful.

**CHORUS**
While Yoshitsugu was going along in the fields and on the mountains we set many spies to take him.

**KUMASAKA**
Let us say that he is come to the village of Ubasike. This is the best place to attack him. There are many ways to escape if we are defeated, and he has invited many guests and has had a great feast at the inn.

**PRIEST**
When the night was advanced the brothers Yoshitsugu and Nobutaka fell asleep.

**KUMASAKA**
But there was a small boy with keen eyes, about sixteen or seventeen years old, and he was looking through a little hole in the partition, alert to the slightest noise.

**PRIEST**
He did not sleep even a wink.

**KUMASAKA**
We did not know it was Ushiwaka.

**PRIEST**
It was fate.

**KUMASAKA**
The hour had come.

**PRIEST**
Be quick!

**KUMASAKA**
Have at them!

**CHORUS (describing the original combat, now symbolized in the dance)**
At this word they rushed in, one after another. They seized the torches; it seemed as if gods could not face them. Ushiwaka stood unafraid; he seized a small sword and fought like a lion in earnest, like a tiger rushing, like a bird swooping. He fought so cleverly that he felled the thirteen who opposed him; many were wounded besides. They fled without swords or arrows. Then Kumasaka said, 'Are you the devil? Is it a god who has struck down these men with such ease? Perhaps you are not a man. However, dead men take no plunder, and I'd rather leave this

truck of Yoshitsugu's than my corpse.' So he took his long spear and was about to make off.

**KUMASAKA**

—But Kumasaka thought—

**CHORUS (taking it up)**

What can he do, that young chap, if I ply my secret arts freely? Be he god or devil, I will grasp him and grind him. I will offer his body as sacrifice to those whom he has slain. So he drew back, and holding his long spear against his side he hid himself behind the door and stared at the young lad. Ushiwaka beheld him, and holding his sword at his side he crouched at a little distance. Kumasaka waited likewise. They both waited, alertly; then Kumasaka stepped forth swiftly with his left foot, and struck out with the long spear. It would have run through an iron wall. Ushiwaka parried it lightly, swept it away, left volted. Kumasaka followed and again lunged out with the spear, and Ushiwaka parried the spear-blade quite lightly. Then Kumasaka turned the edge of his spear-blade towards Ushiwaka and slashed at him, and Ushiwaka leaped to the right. Kumasaka lifted his spear and the two weapons were twisted together. Ushiwaka drew back his blade. Kumasaka swung with his spear. Ushiwaka led up and stepped into shadow.

Kumasaka tried to find him, and Ushiwaka slit through the back-chink of his armour; this seemed the end of his course, and he was wroth to be slain by such a young boy.

**KUMASAKA**

Slowly the wound—

**CHORUS**

—seemed to pierce; his heart failed; weakness o'ercame him.

**KUMASAKA**

At the foot of this pine tree—

**CHORUS**

He vanished like a dew.

And so saying, he disappeared among the shades of the pine tree at Akasaka, and night fell.

# KAGEKIYO

## A PLAY IN ONE ACT

BY

MOTOKIYO

# KAGEKIYO
# A PLAY IN ONE ACT,
# BY
# MOTOKIYO

## PERSONS OF THE PLAY

| | |
|---|---|
| SHITE | Kagekiyo old and blind |
| TSURE | Hime his daughter, called also Hitomaru |
| TOMO | Her attendant |
| WAKI | A villager |
| CHORUS | |

The scene is in Hinga.

# KAGEKIYO

**HIME AND TOMO (chanting)**

What should it be; the body of dew, wholly at the mercy of wind?

**HIME**

I am a girl named Hitomaru from Kamega-engayatsu,
My father, Akushichi-bioye Kagekiyo,
Fought by the side of Heike,
And is therefore hated by Genji.
He was banished to Miyazaki in Hinga,
To waste out the end of his life.
Though I am unaccustomed to travel,
I will try to go to my father.

**HIME AND TOMO (describing the journey as they walk across the bridge and the stage)**

Sleeping with the grass for our pillow,
The dew has covered our sleeves.
(singing)
Of whom shall I ask my way
As I go out from Tagami province?
Of whom in Totomi?
I crossed the bay in a small hired boat
And came to Yatsuhashi in Mikawa:
Ah when shall I see the City-on-the-cloud?

**TOMO**

As we have come so fast, we are now in Miyazaki of Hinga.

It is here you should ask for your father.

**KAGEKIYO (in another corner of the stage)**

Sitting at the gate of the pine wood, I wear out the end of my years. I cannot see the clear light, I know not how the time passes. I sit here in this dark hovel, with one coat for the warm and the cold, and my body is but a frame-work of bones.

**CHORUS**

May as well be a priest with black sleeves. Now having left the world in sorrow, I look upon my withered shape. There is no one to pity me now.

**HIME**

Surely no one can live in that ruin, and yet a voice sounds from it. A beggar perhaps, let us take a few steps and see.

**KAGEKIYO**

My eyes will not show it me, yet the autumn wind is upon us.

**HIME**

The wind blows from an unknown past, and spreads our doubts through the world. The wind blows, and I have no rest, nor any place to find quiet.

**KAGEKIYO**

Neither in the world of passion, nor in the world of colour, nor in the world of non-colour, is there any such place of rest; beneath the one sky are they all. Whom shall I ask, and how answer?

**TOMO**

Shall I ask the old man by the thatch?

**KAGEKIYO**

Who are you?

**TOMO**

Where does the exile live?

**KAGEKIYO**

What exile?

**TOMO**

One who is called Akushichi-bioye Kagekiyo, a noble who fought under Heike.

**KAGEKIYO**

Indeed? I have heard of him, but I am blind, I have not looked in his face. I have heard of his wretched condition and pity him. You had better ask for him at the next place.

**TOMO (to Hime)**

It seems that he is not here, shall we ask further? (they pass on)

**KAGEKIYO**

Strange, I feel that woman who has just passed is the child of that blind man. Long ago I loved a courtezan in Atsuta, one time when I was in that place. But I thought our girl-child would be no use to us, and I left her with the head man in the valley of Kamega-engayatsu; and now she has gone by me and spoken, although she does not know who I am.

**CHORUS**

Although I have heard her voice,
The pity is that I cannot see her.
And I have let her go by

Without divulging my name.
This is the true love of a father.

**TOMO (at further side of the stage)**
Is there any native about?

**VILLAGER**
What do you want with me?

**TOMO**
Do you know where the exile lives?

**VILLAGER**
What exile is it you want?

**TOMO**
Akushichi-bioye Kagekiyo, a noble of Heike's party.

**VILLAGER**
Did you not pass an old man under the edge of the mountain, as you were coming that way?

**TOMO**
A blind beggar in a thatched cottage.

**VILLAGER**
That fellow was Kagekiyo. What ails the lady? she shivers.

**TOMO**
A question you might well ask. She is the exile's daughter. She wanted to see her father once more, and so came hither to seek him. Will you take us to Kagekiyo?

**VILLAGER**
Bless my soul! Kagekiyo's daughter. Come, come, never mind, young miss. Now I will tell you, Kagekiyo went blind in both eyes, and so he shaved his crown and called himself 'The Blind man of Hinga.' He begs a bit from the passers, and the likes of us keep him; he'd be ashamed to tell you his name. However, I'll come along with you, and then I'll call out, 'Kagekiyo;' and if he comes, you can see him and have a word with him. Let us along, (they cross the stage, and the villager calls) Kagekiyo, Oh there, Kagekiyo!

**KAGEKIYO**
Noise, noise! Someone came from my home to call me, but I sent them on. I couldn't be seen like this. Tears like the thousand lines in a rain storm, bitter tears soften my sleeve. Ten thousand things rise in a dream, and I wake in this hovel, wretched, just a nothing in the wide world. How can I answer when they call me by my right name?

**CHORUS**

Do not call out the name he had in his glory. You will move the bad blood in his heart, (then taking up Kagekiyo's thought) I am angry.

**KAGEKIYO**

Living here....

**CHORUS (going on with Kagekiyo's thought)**

I go on living here, hated by the people in power. A blind man without his staff, I am deformed, and therefore speak evil; excuse me.

**KAGEKIYO**

My eyes are darkened.

**CHORUS**

Though my eyes are dark I understand the thoughts of another. I understand at a word. The wind comes down from the pine trees on the mountain, and snow comes down after the wind. The dream tells of my glory, I am loth to wake from the dream. I hear the waves running in the evening tide, as when I was with Heike. Shall I act out the old ballad?

**KAGEKIYO (to the villager)**

I had a weight on my mind, I spoke to you very harshly, excuse me.

**VILLAGER**

You're always like that, never mind it. Has anyone been here to see you?

**KAGEKIYO**

No one but you.

**VILLAGER**

Go on, that is not true. Your daughter was here. Why couldn't you tell her the truth, she being so sad and so eager. I have brought her back now. Come now, speak with your father. Come along.

**HIME**

O, O, I came such a long journey, under rain, under wind, wet with dew, over the frost; you do not see into my heart. It seems that a father's love goes when the child is not worth it.

**KAGEKIYO**

I meant to keep it concealed, but now they have found it all out. I shall drench you with the dew of my shame, you who are young as a flower. I tell you my name, and that we are father and child; yet I thought this would put dishonour upon you, and therefore I let you pass. Do not hold it against me.

**CHORUS**

At first I was angry that my friends would no longer come near me. But now I have come to a time when I could not believe that even a child of my own would seek me out.

(singing)
Upon all the boats of the men of Heike's faction
Kagekiyo was the fighter most in call,
Brave were his men, cunning sailors,
And now even the leader
Is worn out and dull as a horse.

**VILLAGER (to Kagekiyo)**
Many a fine thing is gone, sir; your daughter would like to ask you....

**KAGEKIYO**
What is it?

**VILLAGER**
She has heard of your old fame in Uashima. Would you tell her the ballad?

**KAGEKIYO**
Towards the end of the third month it was, in the third year of Juei. We men of Heike were in ships, the men of Genji were on land. Their war-tents stretched on the shore. We awaited decision. And Noto-no-Kami Noritsune said: 'Last year in the hills of Harima, & in Midzushima, and in Hiyodorigoye of Bitchiu, we were defeated time and again, for Yoshitsine is tactful and cunning.' 'Is there any way we can beat them?' (Kagekiyo thought in his mind) 'This Hangan Yoshitsine is neither god nor a devil, at the risk of my life I might do it.' So he took leave of Noritsune and led a party against the shore, and all the men of Genji rushed on them.

**CHORUS**
Kagekiyo cried, 'You are haughty.' His armour caught every turn of the sun. He drove them four ways before them.

**KAGEKIYO (excited and crying out)**
Samoshiya! Run, cowards!

**CHORUS**
He thought, how easy this killing. He rushed with his spear-haft gripped under his arm. He cried out, 'I am Kagekiyo of the Heike.' He rushed on to take them. He pierced through the helmet vizards of Miyonoya. Miyonoya fled twice, and again; and Kagekiyo cried, 'You shall not escape me!' He leaped and wrenched off his helmet. 'Eya!' The vizard broke and remained in his hand and Miyonoya still fled afar, and afar, and he looked back crying in terror, 'How terrible, how heavy your arm!' And Kagekiyo called at him, 'How tough the shaft of your neck is!' And they both laughed out over the battle, and went off each his own way.

**CHORUS**
These were the deeds of old, but oh, to tell them! To be telling them over now in his wretched condition. His life in the world is weary, he is near the end of his course. 'Go back,' he would say to his daughter. 'Pray for me when I am gone from

the world, for I shall then count upon you as we count on a lamp in the darkness ... we who are blind.' 'I will stay,' she said. Then she obeyed him, and only one voice is left.

We tell this for the remembrance. Thus were the parent and child.

**END**

# NOTES

Ernest Fenollosa has left this memorandum on the stoicism of the last play: I asked Mr. Hirata how it could be considered natural or dutiful for the daughter to leave her father in such a condition. He said, 'that the Japanese would not be in sympathy with such sternness now, but that it was the old Bushido spirit. The personality of the old man is worn out, no more good in this life. It would be sentimentality for her to remain with him. No good could be done. He could well restrain his love for her, better that she should pray for him and go on with the work of her normal life.'

Of the plays in this book, 'Nishikigi' has appeared in 'Poetry,' 'Hagoromo' in 'The Quarterly Review,' and 'Kumasaka,' in 'The Drama;' to the editors of which periodicals I wish to express my acknowledgment.

EZRA POUND.

**Lector House believes that a society develops through a two-fold approach of continuous learning and adaptation, which is derived from the study of classic literary works spread across the historic timeline of literature records. Therefore, we aim at reviving, repairing and redeveloping all those inaccessible or damaged but historically as well as culturally important literature across subjects so that the future generations may have an opportunity to study and learn from past works to embark upon a journey of creating a better future.**

**This book is a result of an effort made by Lector House towards making a contribution to the preservation and repair of original ancient works which might hold historical significance to the approach of continuous learning across subjects.**

**HAPPY READING & LEARNING!**

LECTOR HOUSE

**LECTOR HOUSE LLP**
**E-MAIL: info@lectorhouse.com**

9 789356 146778

Printed by Libri Plureos GmbH in Hamburg,
Germany

9 789356 146778